INNER ALIGNMENT

INNER ALIGNMENT

Authenticity, leadership & living your most powerful life

DINESH SENAN

OPENBOOK CREATIVE

Om Kriya Babaji Nama Aum

For the lights of my soul

Nishant, Niraad & Nikhil

&

For the gift of my life

Shiva & Senan

&

For the joys of my heart

Afsoon, Amanda, Angel, Balraj, Brian, Bruce, Carl, Dina, Haresh, Jacintha, Jin, Lena, Minu, Sajen, Sidhan, Sonny, Sugidha & Suresh

An inspired and uplifting work

Dr Deepak Chopra,
Author, Physician and Mind, Body & Spirit Wellness Expert

Inner Alignment *clearly shows the linkages between the inner alignment of our personal energy expenditures and our ability to achieve higher levels of true authenticity. As Dinesh Senan points out, not to harness the energy flowing into us results in a less than optimized human experience. And who would want that?*

Inner Alignment *is enhanced by the stunning art of Pavarthi Nayar, a beautiful collection of paintings that prompt the reader to pause and reflect on both the work of the artist and the words just read.*

Read this book. Reflect upon its message. You'll find yourself with a greater sense and understanding of how to live the remainder of your life.

Steven Howard,
Co-Editor, *Project You: Living A Determined Life*

Dinesh Senan captures the vital and subtle connections between our inner alignment of thoughts and feelings with the outward alignment we experience in our lives. This delightful book offers a fresh view of the journey to authentic leadership from the inner alignment of our source to the outer alignment of our influence and possibilities in the world.

Ron Kaufman
New York Times bestselling author of *Uplifting Service*

Dinesh's book is a sheer delight. Not only has he a rare gift with words, he also makes us a gift by sharing with us this lucid account of his own personal, transformational journey towards relearning authenticity and becoming an enlightened leader.

>Martin J Kleinelanghorst
>Renewable Energy Technological & Financial Engineering Specialist

Inner Alignment captured my heart and mind and I align myself to the fundamental and simple principles it advocates in today's hyper digital world. This book enlightened my fundamental beliefs in Authenticity, Rhythm and Energy in Leadership and has further strengthened my resolve and conviction to soldier on with Love and Energy and to let the Soul lead me. Simply soulful and simply brilliant!!!

>Barathan Pasupathi
>CEO of Jetstar Asia airline

Published in 2015 in Australia by Dinesh Senan

dinesh.senan@via-group.com
www.via-group.com

Text copyright © Dinesh Senan 2015

Book Production:	OpenBook Creative
Illustrations:	Parvathi Nayar
Editor:	Lu Sexton

Dinesh Senan asserts his moral right to be identified as the author of this book.

All rights reserved.
No part of this publication may be reproduced, stored in a retrieval system or transmitted in any form or by any means electronic, mechanical, photocopying, recording or otherwise is without the prior written consent of the publisher. The only exception is by a reviewer, who may quote short excerpts in a review.

Australia Cataloguing-in-Publication entry

Author:	Senan, Dinesh, author.
Title:	Inner alignment : Authenticity, leadership & living your most powerful life

ISBN:
9781925144246 (hardback)
9781925144253 (ebook)

Subjects:	Soul
	Emotions
	Energy psychology
	Mind and body
	Self-actualization (Psychology)
	Spiritual life
	Introspection

Other Creators/Contributors:

Nayar, Parvathi, illustrator.

Dewey Number:	158.1

Disclaimer: Although the author and publisher have made every effort to ensure that the information in this book was correct at press time, the author and publisher do not assume and hereby disclaim any liability to any party for any loss, damage, or disruption caused by errors or omissions, whether such errors or omissions result from negligence, accident, or any other cause.

CONTENTS

1. The Body as Energy — 1
2. Our Beacons of Energy — 5
3. The Two Fundamental Motives of our Energy Radiation: Giving (Love) versus Taking (Fear) — 11
4. Does a Universal Preference for the *Direction* of our Energy Radiation Exist? — 15
5. The Direct Impact of our Energy Radiations upon the World we Create Around us — 21
6. Attaining the First Level of Wisdom: Inner Alignment of our Energy Radiation — 27
7. Attaining the Second (Deeper) Level of Wisdom — 33
8. Just What is this Magical Place we call the Soul? — 43
9. Leveraging our Soul's Directional Dynamic: Life is Giving is Love — 49
10. The Leap of Faith: Let Go, and Let God — 55
11. A Service-centric Life Examined: Our Highest Calling? — 61
12. The Three Magical Catalysts: Joy, Grace & Gratitude — 69
13. Going Beyond: Unleashing the Power of 'Outward Alignment' through Authentic Leadership & Influence — 77
14. Putting it All into Action - Practical Frame of Reference. — 83
15. A Powerful Way to Start our Day — 89
    Acknowledgements — 97

FOREWORD

Few of us can overcome the general fact that we live our lives mired in unhappiness. We may put on a brave face and pretend otherwise to those around us because we are outwardly seeking sources for some measure of fleeting joy. Sometimes, we cannot escape from the solitude of our innermost thought. We tremble at the realization that our uncontrolled and unaligned minds can be our worst enemy because it is ever-present.

I am often asked how it is possible to live a joyful life centered in higher consciousness and absorbed in spiritual bliss. My response is that it will take a lifetime of effective spiritual practice together with the grace of our True Being and a competent and compassionate guide.

However, to paraphrase the words of the great yogi, Paramhansa Yogananda, "there are many paths to the top of the mountain but once you are there, the view is the same." The author of this book, Dinesh Senan, is seeking through his own experiential insights to provide the reader with a road-map to a joyful and grace-filled existence. Demonstrating the effectiveness of such an ambitious and inspiring endeavor would demand the passage of time and the collection of practical results.

What I offer as a recommendation is that when I read *Inner Alignment,* I found much that resonated with the universal appeal of the great masters of the past. Furthermore, the paintings by Parvathi Nayar brought visual impact to the words, and provoked a re-organization of mental patterns.

In these times when all our focus seems to be on physical perfection and postural correctness, it is timely to strike a balance by turning inwardly to the vast but neglected inner alignment of awareness, speech and action. Such a re-focus will lead in due time to an integration of the body-mind-soul complex.

Dinesh and I both share a devotion and surrender to the Divine working in and around us in the person of an immortal being called Mahavatar Babaji – "Om Kriya Babaji Nama Aum".

Om is the expression of the Divine within our body-mind-soul. When we open our awareness and listen to this divine guidance, our actions become Kriya – action that is grounded in awareness and alignment with the Divine. Our actions then become the selfless service that we foster by our devotion to the divine manifestation called Babaji to whom we bow and express our gratitude with Nama. The universal Divine in which all beings are grounded is known as Aum.

It is my sincere hope that this book by Dinesh will move more of our brothers and sisters to enter the path of joy and service.

- Rudra Shivananda
- *(Author, Triple Acharya Yogi & Spiritual teacher, and a Disciple of the Nath Master Yogiraj Siddhanath. Shivananda has worked for 28 years in high tech work in Silicon Valley. He holds a Master of Science degree in Electrical Engineering and a Juris Doctor degree in Law. Since 1988, he has conducted spiritual initiations and led workshops around the world.)*

PREFACE

Dear Reader,

I'm delighted that you have picked this up! Thank you.

With this book I have attempted to present a framework within which may lie a way for us to reclaim our authenticity and influential power in life. And, re-armed with these terrific assets, perhaps to also reclaim our essential ability to be happy and to succeed.

When I first started writing this book, it was an attempt at finding lucidity in the midst of confusion. This was my way of striving to pull myself out of a sea of darkness that had seemingly swallowed up virtually every ray of light in my life. Nothing seemed to be working, despite all of my good intentions. I was drowning, and I was sad.

It was in the midst of this despair that I began to feel a pull 'inwards', deeper into myself than I had ever been drawn before. This journey was driven by a vague sense that that was the only place from which real change could manifest, and a deepening realization that it was about the only realm in this world in which one could be in effective 'control'.

As I reflected, and scribbled down more notes, things soon started to crystallise. Strands of seemingly disparate notions and snippets of borrowed wisdom distilled from earlier decades of discussions, lectures attended and from fairly copious readings in science, religion, business philosophy and spirituality, all magically started to draw together, to galvanise the whole exploratory effort, to take shape, and finally, to make unified and pragmatic sense.

For instance, in the process, one of the key things I began to more fully appreciate was how the mind naturally comes from fear, and that this natural tendency of the mind continually causes the goal-posts of happiness to shift. Even if we do arrive at our original goal, it is never truly quite sufficient once we've actually arrived! The result being that when we come from the mind, we effectively place the attainment of happiness at risk!

I began to feel, as I progressed, that a certain re-setting of sorts, of my own 'internal compass', was necessary. And way overdue! In the course of these writings, interspersed with some delicious pauses gratefully savoured along the way, I permitted myself to deeply reflect upon some of these less tangible notions, and the 'pathway' that then emerged quite literally lit up and began to totally transform the very fabric of my life.

What I had initially wrestled with was my deeply ingrained mode of 'mind-led' thinking - the strict tenets of logic and reasoning imparted by our formal education. This mode of thinking has strong value in that it helps us make useful sense of the world around us; the logical process of rational validation enables us to enjoy the resulting enhanced predictability of the world. Over time however, it began to dawn upon me that there might also be another valid pathway that could lead to fairly reliable predictability of outcome - emerging not just from a certain mode of *thinking*, but from a certain mode of *being*.

This mode of being was, in effect, a new starting point of my every engagement with the world, where rational thinking was never abandoned but relegated through conscious choice, to a secondary role of executing the choices made from a far deeper place than our rational thinking minds. It represented for me a major inner transformation.

This transformation is still very much a 'work-in-progress' for me, and shall remain so till the day I die... and the journey is so much sweeter already!

The resultant insight may simply be summarised as follows: that the pathway to our authenticity, influence and success in life needs to begin with our strictly individual quest for the 'internal alignment' of our energy. This is the easily overlooked yet absolutely critical *starting point* of our outward journey in life. Whenever this inner alignment is fully achieved, in *all* areas of our lives, it leads irrepressibly to our highest state of *authentic* being. And this is the state of being that unfailingly renders us most powerfully *influential* when we purposefully interact and align outwardly with others, without whose energies we could never be sustainably successful. And the great news is that it all begins with something inherently controlable – our own inner alignment – which is nothing more than a refreshing, self-aware *choice* we consistently make!

Ultimately, this book is a wake-up call to service-oriented action, and for all of us to consciously choose to move to a different rhythm in our lives ... our very deepest personal rhythm of who we *truly* are.

Unlike other 'mind-led' approaches, however, the framework presented herein is subtle, and requires a contrarian view on the use of the mind. Much unlearning of customary notions relating to the positioning of the exalted mind, relative to the soul, may well be required, as we allow the soul to reclaim leadership in direction-setting of our lives.

Close friends have insisted this set of notes be shared with others. Hence this book which is now in your worthy hands. These notions have happily helped me to change my life's outlook ... and I do believe they will work for you, too!

With love,

Dinesh Senan,

Singapore, July 2015

In gratitude towards the following patrons of this effort, without whose spirited energy this book might not have materialized:

Dr. Afsoon Ghazvinian

Damien Sidhanand

Guy Vincent

Jeyaratnam P

Joyce Lim

Kelven Tan

Manmindar Singh

Michael Reede

Raina Chua

Ravi Ravindran

Ron Kaufman

Rajnish Puri

Sanjay Sehgal

Sanjay Kuttan

Shanti Bhattacharya

Sanjay Goel

Sugidha Nithiananthan

A Message from our Sponsors

I would personally like to thank the sponsors of *Inner Alignment*, without whose generous encouragement and support, the publishing of this book would not have been possible:

"Inner Alignment ... my wish for its constant presence in adjudication within the administration of justice."

> DAMODARA PARTNERS LLP (Gold Sponsor)
> Suresh Damodara
> *Senior Advocate & Solicitor, and Officer of the*
> *Supreme Court of Singapore.*

"For the beautiful people of Nigeria"

> H.E. The Hon. Mr Haresh Aswani (Silver Sponsor)
> *Singapore's Honorary Consul-General to the*
> *Federal Republic of Nigeria*

INTRODUCTION

Nothing in this book, save for the assertion that our bodies, thoughts, speech and actions are all formed from the same common property known as energy, should be treated as factual.

Everything presented here ought to be subject to the personal test of our private experiential validation. Experience is the deepest reason we have taken our human form: to move beyond merely knowing who we are, to having a richly textured experience of our truest selves.

This book is a gentle invitation to your soul, to give yourself permission to take a 'time-out', to reflect upon the settings of your innermost compass, and to ask if you feel you are truly living your life authentically, and most powerfully.

How often do we find our mind-led lives failing to yield a lasting sense of fulfillment and happiness? How often do we take delightful, yet all too brief, sojourns into the realm of spiritual healing (attending seminars, practicing meditation, etc.) only to find when we return to our harried lives, that nothing has really changed for us?

Also, particularly as we age, how many of us detect a gnawing inner sense of not having lived our truest lives, of not having expressed from the core of our being, from our souls - the very deepest source of our individual authenticity. As a result how often have we been left despondent, with a growing inner dissatisfaction on both frontiers of the mind and of the soul?

This book attempts to provide a framework straddling soul, mind and body. I hope it helps demonstrate how these fundamental elements of your being might harmonise, optimally and pragmatically, as you go about living your daily life, seeking both fulfillment and lasting happiness.

Touch both polarities across the wide spectrum of this transient material life. Reflect, detect and identify with the inner zones of resonance, or feel the dissonance in your soul and find your own innermost validation of the ideas presented in this book - experientially.

1. THE BODY AS ENERGY

Our deepest fear is not that we are inadequate. Our deepest fear is that we are powerful beyond measure.[1]
Marianne Williamson

$E = mc^2$. The elegance of this scientific equation lies in its simplicity. And yet its ramifications are profoundly staggering. It boldly reveals that ALL MASS is ENERGY. This means that everything in the universe – the planets, the stars, the plants, trees and animals, even you – is made of this same property: energy. Energy is your truest, most essential form. It is measurable and quantifiable and is expressed in a multiplicity of forms, wave and particulate matter alike. This includes our very thoughts, whose waves are an expression of measurable energy.

The fundamental difference between these various forms of energy is their frequency of vibration. This is a complex and daunting subject, but for our purposes here, it is enough for us to understand that thought waves occupy the higher frequency end of the universal energy spectrum, and solid matter resides at the lower levels.

In our immediate material experience, it may be understood that all human-made matter was first a thought. An architect's idea is penned onto paper, then progressively 'coalesces' into material form as the plans are realised. From an energy perspective, the energy frequency of the architect's thought, once released through her mind, 'slows down' sequentially, eventually coalescing as a physical building within our perception and awareness. The same is true for your watch, your car and, possibly by extension, for the entire physical universe itself, from the mind of God the creator.

The quantum of energy contained within your individual body alone is staggering. It has been estimated that the amount of nuclear energy that could be released from the cells of an average 80kg human body is almost enough energy to power the entire United States for a month.[2]

A Thought:

We would do very well to try to better understand how to harness and tap into this rich field of energy, sensibly and effectively, whilst journeying through this transient human experience.

ENDNOTES

[1] Marianne Williamso, *Return to Love*, 1992

[2] (Calculation: $E=mc^2$ => $80*9*10^{16}$ = 7.2 exajoules. US total use of energy per annum, from all sources and for all uses, is placed at about 100 exajoules: see The Physics Teacher, Vol 49, Nov 2011, Prof H C Hayden, University of Connecticut).

2. OUR BEACONS OF ENERGY

Let's begin with a contemplation of the objective of our human life.

Our lives within this material world, characterised so wonderfully and dramatically by dualities and polarities, have a core purpose: to enable us to freely touch either polarity, (good versus evil, right versus wrong, sinner versus saint, light versus dark, etc.), and to then reflect upon the resulting inner 'stories' and emotions that ensue. Typically, these are played out in our inner dialogues within our minds, before being more deeply *felt* within our souls. It is through such dialogues and stories that we get to find what resonates – or doesn't – within the recesses of our souls ... an experiential, fantastic journey of self-realisation.

This unending process ultimately shapes us, giving us a finer sense of who we are at the level of our innermost selves. This experiential sense of who we are by far transcends any glib sense of merely 'knowing' who we are, or who we think we are. With this process, we 'evolve' within our lifetime at the core level of appreciating who we truly are. This process of experiential and evolutionary self-realisation is quite possibly the ultimate *raison d'être* of our human existence.

Let's also look at this from an energy perspective. In the short period of time that we choose to don this material human body, and before we step out of it back into our primordial, eternal, energetic state of being, we consume varying quantities of energy, and expend it in numerous ways. This period typically lasts about 80 or so years, a human lifetime. Over the course of this lifetime, we will expend this consumed energy through a number of important 'energy radiating beacons'.

These energy beacons are categorised as follows:

OUR MIND
>The verb of the mind being to THINK; we radiate energy through our **thoughts.**

OUR BODY
>The verb of the body being to DO; we radiate energy through our words and our **deeds.**

OUR SOUL
>The verb of the soul being simply to BE; we radiate energy through our **feelings** (which include our emotions and intuition).

Each of these is powerful, radiating energy, streaming at varying frequencies, from our bodies into the ether that surrounds us. All of these radiations, (thoughts, words, deeds and feelings), are detected by the living

'I count life just a stuff. To try the Soul's strength on.'[3]

Robert Browning, 1812 – 1889

Universe and her 'receptors' – including the other sentient beings within it[4] – consciously or otherwise. This is the matrix of oneness, where unity across all sentient beings actually happens, and is the medium within which cause and effect dance their eternal dance with unlimited potential and creativity. This matrix, as a deeper and more fundamental order of reality, is analogous to the Implicate Order as propounded and described by theoretical quantum physicist David Bohm, wherein "... space and time are no longer the dominant factors determining the relationships of dependence or independence of different elements. Rather, an entirely different sort of basic connection of elements is possible, from which our ordinary notions of space and time, along with those of separately existent material particles, are abstracted as forms derived from the deeper order."[5]

Consider:

What is most important to reflect upon is that these energy radiations, emanating from our beacons, are effectively the causative essence of the physical reality of our own private worlds. They impact and influence the physical reality that envelopes us, and therefore we create our own reality, not the other way around. This understanding alone is one of the single most powerful revelations known to human kind. To not harness this asset of sheer causative strength, to live reactively in the midst of this physical universe, is to resign and relegate oneself (quite unnecessarily!) to the powerless, potential-wasting position of victimhood.

ENDNOTES

[3] Robert Browning, Men and Women, In a Balcony, 1855

[4] See William L Smith, *The Human Electromagnetic Energy Field: Its Relationship to Interpersonal Communication, Journal of Theoretics, Vol 4-2, 2002*, wherein the author concludes: '... our very consciousness is at least theoretically quantifiable in the sense that physics intends; that our very physical bodies may be aerials that can simultaneously transmit EM energy to and receive EM energy from our physical environment, including to and from other people; and that this energy does indeed influence us as both emotions and thoughts, the latter being particularly focused when discussing the issue of prayer.'

[5] David Bohm, 1917 – 1992, *in Wholeness and the Implicate Order*, 1980.

Notes to Self

3. THE TWO FUNDAMENTAL MOTIVES OF OUR ENERGY RADIATION: GIVING (LOVE) VERSUS TAKING (FEAR)

'All human actions are motivated at their deepest levels by one of two emotions: fear or love.'[6]
Neale Donald Walsch

An energy radiation, in our thoughts, words, deeds or feelings, has only one of two prime motivations: it is either expended in the general direction of *taking* for ourselves, or in the general direction of *giving* to others.

Ponder this statement deeply.

Think for a while of a typical mother and her baby, and you will see what 'giving' being behind her every act for that beloved child means. When a mother gives to her child, think of her state of being as she gives. Try to feel the space from which she is acting.

Giving dwells most comfortably within the domain of *love*. Love is typified by an inner paradigm of abundance and total unity, equality and deep affinity with all other living beings. By contrast, without attaching judgment to the words, *taking* falls typically – but not always – within the wider province of *fear*. Fear is love's polar opposite, characterised by such inner paradigms as insufficiency or scarcity, inadequacy and inferiority.

Prior to each instance of our energy expenditure, whether in thought, word, deed or expression of feeling, we have a fundamental choice. That choice lies simply in our deciding the motive or direction of our impending energy expenditure: we either choose to expend our energy in support of *giving* to another (and so to the world), or in striving to *take* for ourselves.

Dwell on this ... its implications are profound.

Imagine:

If you could see yourself living and loving all others as that mother loves and gives to her child, you will realise that heaven's been right here on Earth all along!

ENDNOTES

[6] Neale Donald Walsch, *Conversations with God: an Uncommon Dialogue, Vol 1*, 1995

4. DOES A UNIVERSAL PREFERENCE FOR THE *DIRECTION* OF OUR ENERGY RADIATION EXIST?

'For it is in giving that we receive…'[7]
St Francis of Assisi, 1181 – 1226AD

A further exploration may then be of interest for each of us to pursue: if energy is *always moving,* does universal energy-flow perhaps have a directional preference? Does it support (in a non-judgmental sense) giving more than taking?

As none of this may, of course, be proven, it may be useful to embark on an experiential test, as follows:

First, draw up a list of about 20 people you know. Then, ask each of them in turn to consider the hypothetical scenario below, and to answer the question that follows.

> Imagine if you will, two aspiring cafe operators, Ms A and Ms B. Assume that they both decide to open their outlets on the same day, directly across the street from each other, which means they share the same target market. Assume too, that they are both equally experienced in this line of business, have identical recipes and culinary skills, use identical ingredients for their identical menus, which offer identical items and at the same prices.
>
> Ms A, a dedicated and very diligent person, rises early in the morning on opening day, and asks herself: 'Who am I? What do I want to achieve?' And she answers herself: 'I am a diligent businesswoman and as my prime duty is to growing my business, I want to maximise my profits for the shareholders of my business'. And off to work she goes...
>
> Ms B, an equally dedicated and diligent person, rises and asks herself on opening day: 'Who am I? What do I want to achieve?' And she answers herself: 'I am a service provider, and I therefore want to ensure I provide my customers the very best value for their dollar, every time they patronise my cafe'. And off to work she goes ... All else being assumed equal, after six months of operations, who do you believe will likely have the greater number of loyal customers, or market share, Ms A or Ms B?

Record the responses you receive. Then reflect upon the implications of your findings.

In my observation, having asked this question many times of different people, I have received a response that points well in excess of ninety percent in favour of Ms B!

Could this significantly one-sided outcome be due to their fundamentally different starting points or prime motivations? Ms A's predilection is for seeking how best she can take from this world, whilst Ms B engages the world from the opposite vantage point of earnestly trying to see how best she can give. *And this makes all the difference.*

Whilst Ms A and Ms B's motivations are not mutually exclusive, it is noteworthy that most people pick the one who has the giving/service orientation as likely to be more successful than the one who earnestly seeks profit alone.

What has been your observation?

An Analogy: Preferred Universal Energy Flow as an 'Invisible Current':

The hypothesis that the Universe may have a preferred direction of flow of energy, in supporting giving as opposed to taking, may be likened to observing two fish into a stream. On the surface the stream may appear to be still, but a current flows beneath. The fish that points against the direction of the current finds that for every three swishes of its tail, it moves three lengths up but is pulled back two. It can indeed make progress, but at considerable cost in terms of effort, stress and energy expenditure. Its experience will be filled with a sense of great resistance. The other fish, pointing in the direction of the current, swishes its tail thrice, and is carried nine lengths by the supporting current; far greater results for a given amount of effort, and with considerably less stress. Its experience will be a prevailing sense of ease in the attainment of its goals.

A Visualisation:

If giving represents the favoured direction or the current in the Universal flow of energy, then visualise this as a possibility:

Every time you give you radiate energy; through your thoughts, words, deeds and feelings, out towards your recipients, and you open a temporary 'vacuum/portal' in your body. As nature abhors a vacuum, the Universe's energy then rushes in through this portal, enabling you to then give all the more.

With your efforts and energy expenditure predominantly focused on giving, this becomes an ever-increasing, virtuous cycle: the more you give, the more supportive energy you draw in, giving you potentially all of the resources you need to succeed in your chosen endeavour.

In the process, as a by-product of this ever-increasing flow of Universal Energy *through* you, you may experience your own personal needs being effortlessly fulfilled.

Taking: The other face of Giving

Taking, when it is not motivated by fear, also has its love-based attributes. The act of taking (with gratitude) allows for the experience of joy in the one who renders the gift or the service.

The relevant question here is who are we 'being' (love or fear), as we give and receive, and what experiences are we co-creating for each other to experience.

What has been your experience?

ENDNOTES

[7] Attributed to St Francis of Assisi, 1181 – 1226 AD, *from The Prayer of St Francis*

5. THE DIRECT IMPACT OF OUR ENERGY RADIATIONS UPON THE WORLD WE CREATE AROUND US

Energy, as we know, is a quantity that can be assigned to every particle and object in the material universe, and it exists in many different forms. All forms of energy are equivalent ... energy in one form can disappear but the same amount of energy will appear in another form.[8]

Energy moves endlessly, impacting on everything irrevocably. As we move through this world, we too need to be acutely aware of the impact that our own energy radiations could have upon the world around us.

Through its resulting impact, every radiation, no matter how gentle, is 'heard' by the physical universe as an order or instruction. All energetic vibration affects all other forms of energy, including 'matter'. In this sense, the material world performs as a strictly obedient servant relative to each of these energetic radiations or instructions. That is, as soon as it detects our energy radiations, it proceeds unquestioningly to manifest the content of these radiations in the real world that surrounds us. Our thoughts directly affect our physical reality around us.

In the field of science, quantum physics reveals that matter takes different forms in accordance with the different vantage points of the observer. That is, the very mindset of the observer has been shown to impact the material form displayed![9]

Consider Also:

Where the radiations are clear and unambiguous, the corresponding physical manifestation is most immediately perceived.

Where the radiations are inconsistent and/or ambiguous, those too are *equally manifested*, bringing apparent chaos and confusion into the immediate material 'reality' of the human emitter and observer of those radiations.

It would benefit us, therefore, to be mindful of this impact, and to carefully choose the intention behind our numerous sources of energy radiations, (through our thoughts, words, deeds and feelings), and then align them all, so the resultant manifestation is most immediate, and effective.

Questions:
How is it that Moses could have parted the Red Sea?
Or Christ have turned the water into wine?
An Answer:
By not having any doubt that they could!

> We need to be aware of the 'sponsoring' thoughts, which are the thoughts behind our leading thoughts, as they too, are heard by the universe as energy radiations, and have equal impact and influence. Consider also that to the extent our sponsoring thoughts are NOT aligned with our leading thoughts, the resulting material manifestation will necessarily be confusion itself!

ENDNOTES

[8] per Hermann von Helmholtz, and see also R. Resnick and D. Halliday (1960), Physics, Section 22-1

[9] see Heisenberg's Uncertainty Principle, the works of Niels Bohr and Wolfgang Pauli, and see contemporary studies on 'The Observer Effect'. Fundamental to contemporary Quantum Theory is the idea that there is no phenomenon until it is observed. Per Alex Paterson: 'The implications of the "Observer Effect" are profound because, if true, it means that before anything can manifest in the physical universe it must first be observed. Presumably observation cannot occur without the pre-existence of some sort of consciousness to do the observing. The Observer Effect clearly implies that the physical universe is the direct result of "consciousness".'

6. ATTAINING THE FIRST LEVEL OF WISDOM: INNER ALIGNMENT OF OUR ENERGY RADIATION

Imagining a sailing ship with four mini-rudders, they had all better be aligned if the ship is to sail smoothly! In similar vein, the four energy radiations being emitted from within each of us had better be aligned if we are to attain success most effectively in our lives.

This suggests that ALL our thoughts, words, deeds and feelings need to be totally aligned and congruent. Persons who achieve this are often described as grounded, or centred and *authentic*. Regardless of whether we agree with them, we sense that *they genuinely and fully believe in what they are saying and doing*, and consequently we feel much power emanating from them.

Some notable examples from our not too distant history:

- Abraham Lincoln
- Nelson Mandela
- Mahatma Gandhi
- Mother Teresa
- Muhammad Ali
- Martin Luther King

Achieving this alignment is the key to achieving maximum efficiency in our energy expenditure, especially in terms of seeking to ensure that our goals are met successfully.

Consider:

How to achieve this inner alignment of our feelings, thoughts, words and deeds is merely a matter of conscious choice. It is not a difficult thing to put into practice at all. The key is to always remember to make this choice!

In practical terms it is as simple as pausing for a moment, just before we enter an important business meeting for instance, to speak inwardly to ourselves ... to ask ourselves to bravely ensure that what we *truly* feel and think, we will unfailingly say and do.

We may be surprised at the ensuing heightened receptivity, which the audience at that meeting displays towards us. Our words will invariably bear the gravitas of sincerity, and have a magnetic effect upon our listeners, drawing them in towards our point of view.

Better yet if we can resolve to make this a positive habit in our lives, perhaps as a regular morning prayer... (see the sample prayer Chapter 15, A Powerful Way to Start our Day).

The consequence of any misalignment of the four energy radiations will invariably be confusion and inefficiency in the resultant material outcomes of such a person's life.

In my own experience, whenever there had been even the slightest degree of misalignment between what I've truly felt and thought about a situation, and what I've said and done about it, it has always been a lot more difficult to persuade my targeted listeners or fellow team members to agree with my position. Somehow, others can always sense, consciously or subconsciously, such misalignment or incongruence. It is *impossible to mask*, at least, not sustainably.

To the extent that we walk through this life without such inner alignment, we correspondingly create for ourselves a world in which our relationships become complicated, our intentions confused, and find our objectives unmet.

Yet merely aligning these four sources of energy expenditure (which brings *efficiency* in the way in which we move through the world) is not quite sufficient to bring a sense of authentic fulfillment in our lives...

7. ATTAINING THE SECOND (DEEPER) LEVEL OF WISDOM

'First say to yourself what you would be; and then do what
you have to do.'[10]
Epictetus, 55 – 135 AD

Now, let's take a step deeper into this realm...

Having achieved alignment of thought, word, deed and feelings, there is a further question to be asked: which of these (if any), ought to *lead* – to set the *direction* in which our ship will sail?

Let's go back to the three beacons and their four energy radiations, and examine how we typically use them…

In the pursuit of happiness our traditional approach has been to employ a paradigm of Think (Mind) ➔ Do (Body) ➔ Be (Soul).

For instance, we tell our children: Study hard in school (Think/Mind) ➔ get a good job and work hard (Do/Body) ➔ and you will be successful and therefore happy (Being/Soul)!

This approach effectively deifies the mind, putting it in the direction-setting leadership position. This leaves our happiness conditional upon the preceding mind and body performances, potentially putting it at risk! Furthermore, within this paradigm, our mental goalposts tend to shift so we keep putting off being happy until further 'preconditions' are met (e.g. more business growth and expansion, after which I will *surely* be happy… *tomorrow*…).

An Alternative Paradigm:

There is another way turn the conventional paradigm around 180 degrees. Try instead:

Be (Happy) ➔ Do (Happiest service calling) ➔ Think (How to get more efficient at doing this stuff).

Because you've *started* with a state of *being* – the province of the soul (which reads 'happy'), you are in that state *at the very moment of choosing it*. The soul needs no precondition to be met.

In the very moment you choose to be miserable, you are. In the very moment you choose to *be* happy, you are that too!

Choosing from the soul a happy direction of sail, de-risks our life's happy outcome from that very moment of choice.

An Experiment:

Take a blank piece of paper and look at a tree. In 30 seconds, write down three reasons why it is a beautiful tree. Done? Now turn that sheet of paper over. In the next 30 seconds, write down three reasons why that tree is ugly or displeasing. Done?

Now look at each side of that piece of paper. Notice that whichever side you choose to dwell upon, that can become your reality - you can justify viewing the tree as ugly or, equally, you can justify viewing the tree as beautiful.

In the same way you can choose, in any given moment, to be justifiably sad or happy about what surrounds you. Choosing one or the other determines your state of being, in the very moment of that choice.

'Nothing in life has any meaning except the meaning you give it'[11]

Anthony Robbins

What does your soul choose?

'In this world you've a soul for a compass

And a heart for a pair of wings

There's a star on the far horizon

Rising bright in an azure sky

For the rest of the time that you're given

Why walk when you can fly?'[12]

Mary Chapin Carpenter

Shifting from Think ➔ Do ➔ Be, to Be ➔ Do ➔ Think is a *fundamental inner paradigm shift*. You come henceforth not from a state of thinking or doing but from a more grounded, powerful state of *being* (the verb of the soul). (Hint: we are human 'beings' not human 'doings'...).

This powerful inner shift has the potential to lift your life's game altogether.

One of the consequences of this inner paradigm shift is that we no longer feel the need to come from the space where we have to be 'right', but instead we come from the space where we choose to be happy.

Choosing the direction of sail in my life, not from the mind but from the far quieter place we call the soul, has brought about meaningful change in almost every aspect of my life. Deliberately calming my mind, I am able to hear the softer, more patient, and far wiser voice of my soul.

I live now in a happier place; I perceive my physical surroundings through different eyes, and this has magically drawn towards me more fully–aligned people, strengthened my relationships, attracted stronger resources, and facilitated more happy 'coincidences', than I could have rationally expected, imagined or explained.

'In the attitude of silence, the soul finds the path in a clearer light, and what is elusive and deceptive resolves itself into crystal clearness. Our life is a long and arduous quest after truth, and the soul requires inward restfulness to attain its full height.'[13]

Mahatma Gandhi, 1869 – 1948

Several years ago, Dr Deepak Chopra conducted an interview with one of the world's most successful business leaders, Masaru Ibuka, who was much admired for his instinctive business acumen. Of that interview, Dr Chopra recalls:

> I once interviewed Masaru Ibuka, founder and chairman of Japan's Sony Corp. who was supposed to have great business instincts. I

asked him, 'What is the secret of your success?' He said he had a ritual. Preceding a business decision, he would drink herbal tea. Before he drank, he asked himself, 'Should I make this deal or not?' If the tea gave him indigestion, he wouldn't make the deal. 'I trust my gut, and I know how it works,' he said.

Dr Chopra went on to say:

> Ibuka, at Sony, ...consciously used his intuition and creativity, practiced meditation, and believed in coincidences as a means for opportunity.[14]

Have we really listened to our inner feelings/our souls, and given them their due weight in the decision-making processes of our lives?

'If we become too involved with the objective, external processes of life, we tend to lose touch with perception from the level of our soul. It's when we go within, into an internal quietness as in meditation, we can begin to perceive something which is deeper and more meaningful than just the objective "out there-ness." So it's really important for those of us who have lost touch with our souls to spend some quiet time — not in thinking, not in going over the day's list of everything that has to be done — but in being with yourself in ways that allow a deeper inner reality to bubble up from within your consciousness.'[15]

Fred Alan Wolf, Ph.D. (Theoretical Physics, UCLA)

ENDNOTES

[10] Epictetus, 55 AD – 135 AD, *transcribed by Arrian in The Discourses,* 108 AD

[11] Anthony Robbins, *in The Anthony Robbins Blog, Change Your Life Now,* 2013

[12] Mary Chapin Carpenter, *in her song 'Why Walk when you can Fly',* 1994

[13] Mahatma Gandhi, 1869 – 1948

[14] Dr Deepak Chopra, *recounted in Context Magazine,* 2006

[15] Fred Alan Wolf, Ph.D. (Theoretical Physics, UCLA), *in The Soul and Quantum Physics,* 1998

Notes to Self

8. JUST WHAT IS THIS MAGICAL PLACE WE CALL THE SOUL?

'We all flow from one fountain soul. All are expressions of one love. God does not appear, and flow out, only from narrow chinks and round bored wells here and there in favoured races and places, but He flows in grand undivided currents, shoreless and boundless over creeds and forms and all kinds of civilizations and peoples and beasts, saturating all and fountainizing all.'[16]
John Muir, 1838 – 1914

In Islam, the creation of humans involves God breathing souls into them.[17]

According to Judaism, 'Hashem formed man from the dust of the earth. He blew into his nostrils the breath of life, and man became a living being.'[18]

The present Catechism of the Catholic Church defines the soul as 'the innermost aspect of humans, that which is of greatest value in them, that by which they are most especially in God's image: "soul" signifies the spiritual principle in humans.'[19]

To the Hindu, the existence of the soul (*Atman*) is regarded as self-evident, not needing any proof beyond a simple process of self-enquiry (*Atma Vichara* in Sanskrit). Through *Atma Vichara*, one can come to understand the nature of the soul. The process is one of negating all objective concepts by successively asking oneself the question: 'Who am I?' Going progressively deeper, beyond mere identification with the body, the senses and the thoughts, until all objectivity has ceased, what remains is the pure subjective soul (or the 'self'), *Atman*.[20]

At a very deep level, we know we are not just our bodies. Instinctively we say 'my body'. The possessive pronoun 'my' is telling. Something else – that is you – owns your body.

Authenticity may only be founded upon this very deepest seat of the self. Living with authenticity means living in fullest alignment with the aspirations of your soul.

It is to this space that we must eventually return, if we are to lead a life of deepest fulfillment.

*'Never tell a child 'you have a soul'.
Teach him, you are a soul;
you have a body.'*[21]

George MacDonald, 1824 – 1905

An Exercise:

Take a moment right now to conduct this *Atma Vichara* exercise for yourself... sit quietly with a blank sheet of paper and a pen, and ask yourself the question 'who am I?'

Without distraction, write down the first answer that occurs to you, and then, keep asking yourself the same question, each time writing down your first thought in response to the question.

Try to get to five levels of deeper successive answers.

At what space have you finally arrived?

ENDNOTES

[16] John Muir, 1838 – 1914, *in Bade's Life and Letters of John Muir: Letter to Miss Catherine Merrill,* June 9th, 1872

[17] Holy Qur'an, Part 15, Verse 29

[18] Book of Genesis, Verse 2:7

[19] Catechism of the Catholic Church, para 363

[20] See David Godman, (Editor), *Be As You Are, The Teachings of Ramana Maharshi, Chapter 5,* 1985

[21] George MacDonald, 1824 – 1905, *in the British Friend, a Quaker magazine,* 1892

Notes to Self

9. LEVERAGING OUR SOUL'S DIRECTIONAL DYNAMIC: LIFE IS GIVING IS LOVE

'Love grows by giving. The love we give away is the only love we keep. The only way to retain love is to give it away.'[22]
Elbert Hubbard, 1859 – 1915

Our greatest challenge is one of *un*learning. We need to unlearn how to be mind-led, and to learn instead to be soul-led.

From the time of our childhood, we have been taught to deify our minds.

But the fact is our minds, fearing their own imminent mortality, are perennially fear-filled, especially if left to their own devices.

Our souls, however, being directly connected with God's Universal energy matrix, have no fear. They are eternal, existing before, during and after this transient human body experience. Our souls therefore wear no watches, and speak with the quiet, patient voices of the truly wise.

When we learn to let the soul lead, we can then relegate the mind back to its proper place: one of servitude to the choice of the soul.

This is not to denigrate the mind. The mind will, as a divine blessing, excel in being utilised as a tool of the soul, to focus on devising strategies and plans for the implementation of the soul's choices.

The mind is a poor master, but a grand servant, in the fulfillment of desire.

A Thought:

The soul's only language is the language of love, the strongest force in the Universe.

Love (the verb) is characterised, in its action orientation, by service to others.

Giving to or serving others, especially when done with no expectation of reward, brings to the giver a sense of fulfillment and joy in life that is simply unparalleled. Whilst the giver has no expectation of reward, that does not mean to suggest they should become averse to receiving, as this would thwart someone else's experience of giving. A giver maintains focus on the giving and accepts resources that eventually flow back through their giving state of being, via the Universe's preferred flow of energy.

There is also a direct correlation between the number of people we serve and the degree of happiness we feel in our own lives. This too, lies within the experiential domains of our lives...

Consider:

When we make the shift to the Be Do Think approach, we get to be in loving service to humankind. And we get to come from our very beingness of who we truly are, which is love personified.

Be love, and seek to give to the world

ENDNOTES

[22] Elbert Hubbard, 1859 – 1915, *in The Note Book of Elbert Hubbard, published by Roycrofters,* 1927

Notes to Self

10. THE LEAP OF FAITH: LET GO, AND LET GOD

'If we take even one step forward, Krishna will take ten steps toward us.'[23]
His Divine Grace A C Bhaktivedanta Swami Prabhupada, 1896 - 1977

Allah says 'Take one step toward me, I will take ten steps towards you. Walk towards me, I will run towards you.'[24]

The Prophet Muhammad (s.a.a.w.), c. 570 – 632 AD

> *'Draw near to God and He will draw near to you.'*[25]
>
> James 4:8, *New King James Version of the Holy Bible*

Consider:

The point at which faith or trust in the loving Universe enters this discussion lies in the precise moment when you relinquish the mind from the driver's seat, and place your soul, instead, in the position of directional leadership of your life.

As with all things to do with faith, this is a personal, experiential experiment that each of us can freely decide to embark upon, setting aside for a while any doubts we might have in the process.

Belief that the soul channels our highest pathway is only arrived at some time after we have taken the first steps in truly letting it lead...

Try this for yourself...
It is the longest journey you will ever make in your life,
from your head to your soul.
It is also likely to be a one-way trip!

ENDNOTES

[23] His Divine Grace A C Bhaktivedanta Swami Prabhupada, 1896 - 1977, Founder-Acarya of the International Society for Krishna Consciousness, *in conversation with Atreya Rsi, VedaBase, TD 1-10,* 1976

[24] The Prophet Muhammad (s.a.a.w.), c. 570 – 632 AD, in *Hadith Qudsi*

[25] James 4:8, *New King James Version of the Holy Bible*

11. A SERVICE-CENTRIC LIFE EXAMINED: OUR HIGHEST CALLING?

'I slept and dreamt that life was joy. I awoke and saw that life was service. I acted and behold, service was joy.'[26]
Rabindranath Tagore, 1861 – 1941

Profound changes happen when we start to consciously live our lives along directional lines set by our souls rather than our minds.

We find ourselves moving effortlessly within the Universal flow of energy. That is, in the direction of giving and of service.

The primary focus of our effort will now lie firmly in the service being rendered.

Consequently we are likely, whilst acting in this altered mode of existence, to find that our own material needs are more readily, almost incidentally, taken care of without strenuous effort.

At this juncture, it may be useful for us to consider the fundamental characteristics of the journey typically taken by inner-aligned and soul-directed aspirants:

Living the Service-centric Life:

- **Stage 1: Transcend this Blessed Duality:**

People who have attained this stage seem no longer affected by the duality of the material world... every instance of 'good', 'bad' or 'mixed' outcomes of their actions are treated with equanimity[27] and detachment. They live knowing they are *in* this material world, but not *of* it. They naturally bless each and every outcome in the knowledge that outcomes, at either end of the duality spectrum, serve only in helping define who they truly are or, equally importantly, are not.

'In the state of duality, ruled by the ego, we are powerless subject to the laws of duality and karma. When we begin to recognise that all things are equal, nothing and no one higher or lower, then we move into effortless being and effortless doing. All things we want to experience flow to us.'[28]

Guru Granth Sahib

- **Stage 2: Resolve to Live a Life of Service:**

Having thus transcended the divine drama, they then ask themselves: 'so how shall I most productively spend the remainder of this transient human life?' The inner response they seek, from the level of the soul, would invariably point towards giving (in service) to others.

'Thy business is with the action only, never with its fruits; so let not the fruit of action be thy motive, nor be thou to inaction attached.'[29]

Lord Krishna, c. 3228 – 3102 BCE

'A supreme selflessness characterises the lives of the truly great beings, the central fact of which is a continuous joyous, self-sacrifice for the good of the universe. One may say that the joy of living in their case is purely the joy of living for others. The great value of such lives is that by their achievements they indicate the heights that are attainable by mankind through right effort.'[30]

Sonia Giguère

- **Stage 3: Identify Whom to Serve and in what Form:**

Typically, the next enquiry would be: 'what form of service should this be, and to whom?' The response tends to be: 'to the greatest number of my fellow souls, and through the joyful leveraging of my own core talents and innate skills';

> *'Only a life lived for others is a life worthwhile.'*[31]
>
> Albert Einstein, 1879 – 1955

- **Stage 4: Go with the Soul:**

They then proceed to spend the rest of their lives led by the soul in its supreme state of giving (in service).

Many of the greatest souls who have ever lived have progressed through the four stages above, and proceeded to live extraordinarily impactful lives.

Some notable examples:

- St Francis of Assisi
- The Buddha
- Mother Teresa
- Jesus Christ

Let's resolve to give this a try too. Let us be our own role models in seeking to serve the greatest number of people we possibly can before reaching the end of our human journey. And let's observe the outcomes.

ENDNOTES

[26] Rabindranath Tagore, 1861 - 1941, *as quoted in Jesse Herman Holmes: A Quaker's Affirmation for Man, page 287*, 1951

[27] Lord Krishna, c. 3228 – 3102 BCE, in *The Bhagavad Gita*, Chapter 2, Verse 48

[28] At the beginning of the sacred Sikh text, the Guru Granth Sahib, *within the sacred hymn, Japji Sahib, Stanza 33*, c. 1604

[29] Lord Krishna, c. 3228 – 3102 BCE, *in The Bhagavad Gita, Chapter 2, Verse 47*

[30] Sonia Giguère, *Babaji's Kriya Yoga Centre, California*, 2008

[31] Albert Einstein, 1879 – 1955, *quoted in the New York Times*, 20th June 1932

12. THE THREE MAGICAL CATALYSTS: JOY, GRACE & GRATITUDE

'Success is not something you pursue. What you pursue will elude you. It can be like trying to chase butterflies. Success is something you attract and accumulate by the person you become.'[32]
Jim Rohn, 1930 - 2009

There are almost invariably three additional chosen qualities or attributes of inner-aligned and soul-driven persons, successfully engaged in loving service of their fellow human beings:

- Joy
- Grace
- Gratitude

This is no accident.

These three qualities, when chosen from the level of the soul, will catalyse the speediest attainment of our success during our lifetimes.

Catalysts accelerate reactions. Let's consider why and how these three qualities might serve to accelerate the attainment of our success. Notice the extent of resonance there may, or may not, be within you.

JOY: Joy is a sublime state of happiness, chosen from the core of our being, and independent of our physical surroundings.[33]

Try this: smile as you greet people. Observe how long they then stay around you. Now, try the opposite ... scowl as you greet others. Observe how long they now stay around you. Is there a difference? Chances are, yes. Why? Joy is magnetic. It is attractive and draws others towards you. Others would most naturally wish to bask in your radiant sunshine.

GRACE: Grace is an elegant manner of flowing harmoniously through this journey of life.

Try this: resolve to move gently through this world. Stop and smell the roses. Slow down. Resist the mind's many pseudo-urgent impulses. Sip a cup of tea whilst looking out your window, feet propped up. Get into that deliciously quiet space *between* your thoughts ... allow that space to unfold ... and take comfort in languishing there for a while. Let nothing ruffle your feathers, ever, without your permission. Gracefully connect with the sublime, quiet, wise, unconditionally loving Universal field of energy. Observe the impact of your choosing to do so, on yourself and, on others around you. Do you have more people suddenly showing up in your life, wishing simply to be around you more often?

'Joy is prayer; joy is strength; joy is love; joy is a net of love by which you can catch souls.'

Mother Teresa, 1910 - 1997

> **Consider this possibility:**
>
> Joy and grace are conditions that further amplify the energy field created around the core of your aligned energy radiators (your thoughts, words, deeds and feelings). Just as magnetic fields are created around electrical cores, by living in joy and grace you attain higher 'magnetic' attractiveness, increasing the rate at which Universal energy is drawn THROUGH your inner-aligned self, and enabling you to attain your chosen objectives more efficiently and effectively.

Living in and as grace, consider two hypothetical scenarios:

Imagine a waitress accidentally spilling a glass of juice on your lap when you are having lunch at a restaurant in the middle of a busy day.

Scenario 1: You yell at her and threaten to complain to her manager about her clumsiness and the inconvenience this is now going to cause you. You demand some form of redress for this situation. She is apologetic and afraid she could lose her job, and tries to go about appeasing you...

Scenario 2: You look her in the eyes and say, 'Not to worry, my dear. I'm all right, these things do happen, it's okay...' She is apologetic, rushes to clear the mess and is totally concerned about you, your well-being, and any inconvenience the mishap might have caused you... Inwardly she is grateful you are not threatening to get her into trouble, as she really needs this job...

Chances are that at various times in our lives, and in similar situations, we might have reacted angrily and with self-interest (as in Scenario 1). At other times we might have reacted with empathy, being immediately concerned with putting the waitress at ease (as in Scenario 2).

In the first scenario we are concerned about the problems with which we will be faced – this is fear based. In the second, we are concerned about the waitress, motivated to ensure she doesn't feel bad or worry too much – which is love based.

The latter reaction becomes the customary one, when we consciously choose to live in, and as, grace.

A Reflection:

> *At every juncture in our lives when confronted with a choice of response, let's pause for a moment and ask:*
> *"What would Love do now?"*
> *Even as we ask this question, our highest response immediately becomes self-evident.*

Having experienced ourselves in similar situations, and displaying each of the two reactions in earlier instances over the course of our lives, consider which response resonates more strongly, deep within us? Which type of response better represents our inner sense of who we might be?

And also pause to consider: what does your chosen form of response do to affect the quality of the relationship you now have with the people who bore witness to the event, including the waitress? Is your *personal attractiveness* as a being enhanced or diminished?

GRATITUDE: Of the three catalysts, gratitude is the greatest. It is a great accelerant in our journey of unlearning how to be mind-led, and to learning to be soul-led. This is because gratitude switches us off from the state of *wanting* – a nervous state that turns on the mind, giving its frantic voice even greater power and influence – and switches us instead into a higher vibrational state of *abundance*. Gratitude leaves us smiling at what we already have, and also leaves us smiling in the quiet, confident knowledge that whatever we have called for from the depths of our souls is *already* hurtling towards us in our material reality, in the very moment of our calling. This, incidentally, demonstrates the Universal energy's *unconditional love*.

What *interferes*, however, with the manifestation of our soul's desired outcomes are our conflicting fear-based thoughts, words and deeds. Those too are 'heard' *equally well*, in a non-discriminatory fashion, and dutifully acted upon and manifested within our actual reality by the Universal field of energy. Confused outcomes then necessarily result.

Consider this Paradigm:

Let gratitude be used as a catalyst in helping replace fear-based thoughts, words and deeds. This helps reduce the perceived time-lag between our soul's radiated intentions into the Universe, and their corresponding material manifestation in our reality. This is because gratitude is, fundamentally, the very opposite of being in the state of wanting.

Adopting gratitude as our constant state of being therefore helps remove the many layers of fear-based thoughts and actions of want or lack, which run counter to our desired outcomes.

When we draw closer towards mastery of our inner alignment, whilst choosing to live in and as joy, grace and gratitude, the time-lag between our soul's intentions and their material manifestation diminishes progressively.

Full mastery witnesses instantaneous attraction of all material resources to fulfill our chosen goals.

ENDNOTES

[32] Jim Rohn, 1930 – 2009, (pre-eminent American motivational speaker, entrepreneur and author), *as quoted by Darren Hardy, in The Compound Effect: Jumpstart Your Income, Your Life, Your Success, page 72,* 2011

[33] Mother Teresa, 1910 – 1997, *in A Gift for God,* 1975

What has been your experience in this regard?

13. GOING BEYOND: UNLEASHING THE POWER OF 'OUTWARD ALIGNMENT' THROUGH AUTHENTIC LEADERSHIP & INFLUENCE

'Man is his own star and the soul that can render an honest and perfect man commands all light, all influence, all fate.'[34]
John Fletcher, 1579 – 1625

Achieving directional inner alignment renders us fully authentic.

This authenticity originates from and is led by our souls, the seat of our own *being,* and of our *truth*.

Once attained, this authenticity holds a certain characteristic – a charismatic, magical *magnetism*, which has the galvanizing power to attract, influence and draw resources and other people towards us, whether at the conscious or subconscious levels.

> *Leadership demands the expression of an authentic self ...*
> *people want to be led by someone 'real' ...*[35]

Rob Goffee and Gareth Jones

Authenticity is the external effect of our inner alignment. It carries the power of influence over others.

Such authenticity and influential power helps us to then achieve alignment with another person, as we strive to extend a soul-to-soul 'outward alignment' with that person.

This is the deepest source of sustainable leadership. Here, and to the extent that alignment is achieved across both souls, the synergistic flow of Universal energy through the two aligned souls will be greatly amplified in its combined causative power.

In leading large, multicultural corporate teams over the past three decades, and across many regions of the world, I have seen and learned first-hand the value of influence, and have come to understand its roots in the perception of authenticity of the aspiring leader.

Our greatest success in life can only come through the active collaboration and support of others, fostered through the influential power of the leader.

> *'And the more souls who resonate together the greater the intensity of*
> *their love and, mirror-like, each soul reflects the other...'*[36]

Dante, c. 1265 - 1321

'To be persuasive, we must be believable; to be believable, we must be credible; to be credible, we must be truthful.'[37]

Edward R Murrow, 1908 – 1965

A Thought

At the highest level of abstraction, this combined soul-to-soul alignment across the entire Universe, may be perceived as non-different from God in her supreme causative realm.

Perhaps the greatest consequence of our attaining inner alignment is the enhancement of our ability to more powerfully collaborate with and lead others, through 'outward alignment', anchored sustainably upon our own authenticity.

ENDNOTES

[34] John Fletcher, 1579 – 1625, *in the Jacobean stage play, 'The Honest Man's Fortune'*, 1613

[35] Rob Goffee and Gareth Jones, *Harvard Business Review*, December 2005

[36] Dante, c. 1265 - 1321, *in the Divine Comedy*, 1320

[37] Edward R Murrow, American Journalist, 1908 – 1965, *quoted by Prof. Tom Lambert, in The Power of Influence, Introduction, pg 1,* 1996

14. PUTTING IT ALL INTO ACTION - PRACTICAL FRAME OF REFERENCE.

'Between stimulus and response, there is a space. In that space, our
power to choose our response. In our response lies
our growth and our freedom.'[38]
Viktor E Frankl, 1905 - 1997

When we truly recognise that it's all the same energetic core stuff, that everyone is held within everything else in a quantum field of infinite and interrelated possibility, then will we see just why it is that we need to be conscious of all the energy we channel through us. And why all of our choices, must be in full alignment, with sound direction.

This is because the material stuff we swim in all day, that surrounds us so completely ('our reality'), is always the direct result of how we ourselves manipulate and organise – sensibly or otherwise, consciously or subconsciously – the energy that we were temporarily a steward of, before we release it back into the Universe.

It's when we fully appreciate this - that this is how we cause our own realities – that we will take *utmost care* to ensure that we *choose* not only to align all of our inner energy beacons with precision, but also to have them all pointed optimally in the authentic, soul-led direction in life that will yield our lasting success and happiness.

In Summary

Aligning our inner rudders of thought, word, deed and feelings achieves **efficient sailing**. Choosing feelings (the language of the soul) to take the lead, determines our **optimal direction of sail in life**.

> **4 energy radiators**, (thought, words, deeds, feelings), **via**
>
> **3 beacons**, (mind, body, soul), **with**
>
> **2 fundamental motivations**, (love, fear), **where**
>
> **1 radiator sets the direction of sail** (the soul, in the direction of giving)

Pulling it all together, here is a frame of reference to contemplate:

The 4 A's:

Step 1 : AWARENESS:

Be *aware*, at the level of your feelings, of what brings you the most joy in doing. Choose that area of service to be a provider thereof in this world... that is, always begin by *coming from a state of being that is characterised by 'happiest service giving'*. (Note that in your doing what brings you joy, you will truly be most *authentically you*, and you will thereby be potentially of greatest service value to others.)

Step 2 : ALIGNMENT:

Then, consciously seek to *align* each of your other energy radiations (your thoughts, words and deeds) behind this chosen state of being, such that they consistently serve as your soul's implementation tools.

Step 3 : ACTION:

Now move boldly – coming from, and being, the states of joy, grace and gratitude – into focused *action*. Your soul's chosen direction shall be implemented by your aligned thoughts, words and deeds.

Step 4 : AMAZEMENT:

Now observe in *amazement* as your 'magnetized' core starts to miraculously draw every success resource you ever thought you might need towards you, without limitation. You are now swimming powerfully in the direction of the current of Universal energy flow. Your state of inner alignment is characterised by mounting, inexplicable 'coincidences' and instances of 'synchronicity', as the pieces of the resource jigsaw begin to pop up onto the radar screen of your consciousness.

What has been your experience in this regard?

A Parting Paradigm: Choose from your Soul:

'... use all the resources at your command, all the tools at your disposal, all the insights you can muster, and all the wisdom you can draw to you to re-create yourself and your world anew in the next grandest version of the greatest vision ever you held about who you are ...'[39]

Neale Donald Walsch

ENDNOTES

[38] Viktor E Frankl, 1905 – 1997, in *Man's Search for Meaning*, 1946

[39] Neale Donald Walsch, *Friendship with God: An Uncommon Dialogue*, 2002

15. A POWERFUL WAY TO START OUR DAY

Here is a special, highly potent Morning Prayer that pulls
it all together for us:

O Divine Lord...

Thank you for the great blessing that is this life of mine. Please be with me always and help me, as Your instrument of service here on earth, to heighten my awareness of all that I might feel, and to ensure that all that I might think, that I might say and that I might do today will be fully aligned within me, And also with Your truth and love.

Amen.

I pray it may have some resonance for you too...

Taking just a moment to pause, at the start of our day, or just before our most important encounters with others, to say this little prayer, makes a profound difference in the outcomes that lie ahead. Try it for yourself, and feel the difference, experientially.

About the author *Dinesh Senan*

Dinesh is a strategic business and market development professional with more than 28 years of cross-border experience; serving at regional CEO level within several multinational enterprises - primarily within the communications and energy sectors.

He currently serves as an entrepreneur passionately committed to the promotion, financing and global diffusion of new industrial-scale sustainable energy solutions, working across Asia, Africa, Europe and the Americas. The mission is to sustainably re-invent Man's industrial relationship with our planet.

At every stage of his work-related efforts, and ever since he commenced his spiritual journey more than 20 years ago, Dinesh has attempted to put into real-world practice the ideas and approaches suggested in the book.

For him, the consequences have been profound, and, but for the approaches suggested in the book, otherwise rationally inexplicable. An incredible array of aligned persons across the planet - from the high technology, global finance and transnational operational business world - now work alongside him on this mission, with a wide range of relevant resources popping up, synchronistically, at every turn.

Dinesh now strives to be more aware that we are all spiritual beings temporarily having a human experience, and to live accordingly.

Every day now starts and ends with the prayer suggested at the end of the book. Each new day a surprise-filled opportunity to further practice, and thereby experientially and personally validate the magical principles contained within the book.

About the artist *Parvathi Nayar*

Parvathi is an Indian contemporary visual artist who is known for her drawing and video practices, and as someone who has consistently experimented in her art with different media, concepts and ways of expression.

The drawings in this book are selected from her early experimental series, where colour, texture and forms were the means by which Parvathi sought to explore humanistic concerns in the world. Conceptually her work is rooted in exploring relationships with the world, in ways that privilege sight and encourage viewers to see the world they thought they knew, in new ways.

Parvathi received her Masters in Fine Art from Central St Martins College of Art and Design, London, on a Chevening scholarship. She has exhibited widely and has been collected extensively by institutional, corporate and private collectors around the world.

Parvarthi is a prolific and highly regarded artist, with a drawing and painting practice in Chennai, India. https://www.facebook.com/parvathinayarart

NOTES TO SELF

ACKNOWLEDGEMENTS

Very special thanks are due to Amanda Colliver, for so gently holding me together in the darkest days of my life, and for her infinitely joyful and nurturing wisdom.

A big heartfelt thank you too to Dr Deepak Chopra for his loving friendship and encouragement, and to Sajen Aswani, Bruce Bonny, Louw Burger, Harjinder Dhaliwal, Dr Afsoon Ghazvinian, Priscilla Gopalan, Ronald Howe, Ankya Klay, Ramesh Jude Pachamuthu, Rameish Sivalingam, Greg Spiro, Jacintha Stephens & Kadi Tombak for their invaluable critical and constructive input, which has significantly helped improve the quality of the content of this book.

Warm appreciation is also extended to Parvathi Nayar for collaborating with me to reproduce a selection of her exquisitely beautiful paintings for this book.

A huge debt of gratitude is also owed to Julie Renouf and Lu Sexton of OpenBookCreative in Melbourne, Australia for their highly sensitive and incisively intelligent editorial and publishing skills, which have transformed this work into something far better than I could possibly have rendered alone.

www.ingramcontent.com/pod-product-compliance
Lightning Source LLC
Chambersburg PA
CBHW042330150426
43194CB00001B/8